5 BEST MARKETING STRATEGIES FOR SMALL BUSINESS OWNERS

HOW TO EARN MORE WITHOUT HIRING A MARKETING TEAM

KELLY GAWITT

"You have something truly valuable to offer; solutions that people desire. All you need is a marketing plan and the perfect words."

Kelly Gawitt

Table of Contents

Keep Your Hard-Earned Cash

I'm not one to waste words. You picked up this book because you need help. You need to learn how to market your product or service without wasting your time or money on fluff and flashy gimmicks. So here is what I'm going to do. I'm going to explain in plain English how to implement the exact same marketing strategies I use with my top-paying clients every day.

I'm going to give you the equivalent of a consultation call and a one-on-one coaching call complete with an easy-to-accomplish marketing plan.

Why?

Because I know what it's like to be where you are sitting right now. You're early in your entrepreneurial journey. You're still figuring out all the details, the hundreds of details… and you've only got so much time and energy to devote to researching this stuff. I want to put all the necessary information into your hands right now so you can stop wasting hours on the internet after an already long day of work.

You should be enjoying a beer and your weekends at home, hiking with your dog, or traveling–*not working overtime on marketing!*

If you've been searching for an easy-to-digest *and implement* game plan, you're holding it in your hands. By the time you're done with this book, you'll have the knowledge you need to maximize your earning potential without hiring an expert.

Keep your hard-earned cash!

With so many of us doing more of our business online, knowing how to incorporate digital marketing strategies is a must. For most businesses that involves hiring a marketing team or a marketing specialist who is also a skilled copywriter. Either of those options requires a sizeable marketing budget. It also means parting with your hard-earned cash, and, if we're honest, you're really afraid to let go of your money right now. Right? You've only been a business owner for a short time and you don't have a marketing budget yet.

It's a hard place to be as a small business owner. You know marketing will grow your business, but you're struggling to cover the cost of doing business. Even if you've earned a small profit, you want to keep that in the bank, not give it away.

I get it. I'm in marketing myself and early in my freelancing career I desperately wanted to hire someone to help me, but I couldn't afford to. I was a stay-at-home mom, homeschooling my three kids, and trying to work a side hustle. My husband and I struggled stretching every dollar we had so there was no way I'd spend money on a marketing agency for my small business.

So, just like you, I'd find myself not able to sleep even though I was exhausted at the end of the day. I'd spend hours every night wrestling with those nagging questions, *Can I afford to hire an expert? Can I afford not to? Why can't I figure this out on my own?*

I lost so much sleep, I wasted so much time and so much energy.

After several months of chasing the gurus, reading all that I could online and in books, and watching a ton of YouTube videos by so-called marketing experts I realized something. There is no big secret to marketing.

There isn't.

Everyone was saying the same thing in different ways. Everyone also had something of their own to sell, namely coaching services on how to market your business. And of course, they are promising BIG results.

You'll be earning six figures in no time with my course.

You can finally take that vacation!

No more stress. No more worry. No more wasted time and energy.

Everything you need in one place.

Imagine more time with family, enjoying your weekends again.

Sprinkle in a few great testimonials and tantalizing images of beautiful people smiling on a yacht sipping brightly colored cocktails with succulent tropical fruits skewered onto cute little umbrellas. It's paradise and you want it now! It's your literal dream come true!

That is…until you see the price tag.

You can spend anywhere from a few hundred dollars to thousands of dollars trying to learn how to do your own marketing. But you don't have to.

Behind all the hype, all the pretty smiles and glittering promises, the facts about how to market your business successfully is common knowledge and readily available on the internet or at your local library. Because what is behind effective marketing isn't learning the latest trends on social media. Successful marketing has to do with communicating effectively and persuasively to your prospective audience. What worked 100 years ago still works today.

You have to understand your customer intimately, use a little psychology, and learn how to write copy.

Build Your Email List

Someone just landed on your website! Great. Now what?

Every time someone clicks on your website that means they're interested in what you have to offer. Will they buy in right away? Some will. But the majority of visitors are checking you out. They need time to think through their buying decision. This means they will spend some time on you sight and then click away.

Don't Lose Those Leads

The first thing I always tell my clients is that they must have an enticing offer to get people to sign up for your subscriber list. The reason for this is simple, though not everyone considers it. Once they hear me say it though, their eyes widen as their brows go up and they say, *"Ooooh!"* as they realize how valuable this marketing strategy is. Let me explain the importance of an email list to anyone, any business owner, or entrepreneur who has a website.

Remember when we watched helplessly as social media platforms canceled certain accounts without warning?

Yeah. That's paralyzing to any business.

Facebook, Instagram, TikTok, etc., all these platforms can shut down your accounts or cancel you without notice. And there goes your access to reach all your followers. Social media platforms also change their algorithms causing you to have to jump through new hoops in order to stay relevant to your followers.

Without another way to reach potential customers and clients, we are at the mercy of the conglomerates, forced to do things their way. But you don't have to.

Not if you are actively building and nurturing our own email list.

Now do you see why it's so vital to your business to build an email list?

Your subscriber list is gold!

Your ideal clients give you their permission to show up in their inboxes and keep the conversation going. It's the equivalent of being an invited guest! They invite you into their virtual living rooms and you have permission to sell them your product or service.

That means lots of fresh new leads for your business. Leads that voluntarily come to you from people who are already open to your message. So write to them. Be sure you make the most of this marketing asset wisely.

Do not annoy them with fluff or nonsense. Only send them valuable information. Don't be spammy. Don't be salesy. Don't try to be slick. People can see right through that and they will stop opening your emails or worse—mark you as spam!

Do this instead.

Give your prospective customers a way to sign up for your email list. Offer them a free, super valuable piece of content in exchange for their first name and email address. Every time someone clicks on your website that means their interested in what you have. Don't lose their interest. Build upon it through nurturing emails. I'll cover that in the next chapter.

You can also ask for their last name and phone number but sometimes asking for too much info discourages people from signing up at all. So keep it as simple as possible. The idea is to just get their contact info as quickly and as easily as possible.

Be sure to offer something that's of genuine value. Something that's helpful. Something you'd be willing to give up your address for. Then show up with more value in your nurturing emails to follow. Over-deliver. Give them more help, suggestions, tips, or ideas. Share a personal story where appropriate. They'll love you for it.

Opt-in Options

People always ask me, what kind of opt-in offer should I make? That's a great question! And to answer that we need to do some thinking. First, take a minute and think about this from your ideal clients point of view. What would be helpful or valuable to them?

Secondly, think about what motivates you to give away your email address. What did you exchange it for?

An ebook or a checklist? Maybe it was a guide with tips and tricks on how to solve a particular problem. Or was it a free video course?

The type of free content you have given away your email address for is a good place to start. Also, look around and see what your competitors in your industry are offering. Could you offer something similar or something better?

Bonus Pro Tip

All these types of free opt-in offers can be easily made on <u>Canva</u> or a similar design platform. They have tons of templates to get you started and it's easy to use.

Another tip; slow down when you're scrolling through your social media feeds. What are people trying to sell you? What are they offering to you in exchange for your email address? Consider signing up for some of these freebies just to learn from them.

Then ask yourself, *was it a good offer?*

If not, why? Could you offer something better?

Was it a great offer? If yes, could you create something similar?

There are all kinds of great ideas out there. Generate ideas by assessing your competitors and favorite brands. Consider if their strategies are working and why. Take notes and learn from them.

Email Marketing

This is where the marketing magic happens. Email sequencing is where you have been granted permission to sell to your ideal client. It's true. When they signed up to your subscriber list they essentially invited you into their private space to talk about your offer. This is where you get to position yourself as the knowledgeable and compassionate business person you are–the person with the solution they want and need.

Please do not overlook this marketing strategy. It's vital to the process of growing your business, even if your list is small right now. Over time, as you invest the time and energy to build it, it will grow. When you use email marketing your return on investment is typically $36 for every dollar you spend.

Whether you call them email campaigns, click funnels, or sales funnels or sequences, they mean the same thing. They're the tool that allows you to offer value and build trust with your audience.

But there is some finess involved. After all, no one likes being sold to. You don't want to come across as pushy.

So imagine you've met someone really interesting. They're funny, share your values and they are on the same path as you, only a bit further down the road. You decide that you want to build a friendship and see where it leads. Who knows, maybe they are just the person you need to help you figure something out or at least be encouraging as you try.

You wouldn't say, "Hey, I really like you. Want to be my best friend? Maybe we can have a sleepover this weekend? That would be going way over the line. It's the same with your subscribers. Don't come on too strong.

Making the Most of Your Subscriber List

Start by delivering your freebie offer that enticed them to subscribe and add some encouraging message. Then continue to nurture the relationship. Think of it as going on a series of dates through email.

Invest time in building a meaningful connection. Whether you send emails once a week or three times a week doesn't matter as much as the value and usefulness of the information you provide. Avoid risking their annoyance by spamming or using pushy sales tactics. Instead, offer them help, valuable tips, tricks, ideas, and solutions to their problems.

By doing this, you'll attract a loyal following who appreciates your efforts and shares their positive experiences with others. Your goal is not to sell them anything yet, but rather to educate, inspire, and entice them. Through a well-crafted email sequence, your aim is to make them genuinely like you.

As time goes on, they'll eagerly read your emails, nodding their heads in agreement with your every word. This is where you want to guide them—to a place of trust. As you consistently provide them with useful information, their belief in you will strengthen. When you keep giving them what they need and what they can use. They'll recognize the value and appreciate your generosity.

Serve them without expecting anything in return. After wooing them through a series of emails, you can introduce a small ask. This could be something simple like asking them to share your content on social media, follow you on Instagram, forward to a friend, or post on Pinterest. This will broaden your reach and has the potential to grow your subscriber base.

And for goodness sake, make it easy for them. Include a clickable button that enables them to take the desired action effortlessly. This process is akin to dating, where small gestures, kind acts, thoughtful gifts, and opening doors create a foundation of trust.

The Power of The Small Ask

Be aware that there is a marketing psychology at work in *the small ask*. You initially provided them with a fantastic free offer that was easy to accept—a mere name and email address required, no commitment. People appreciate that. So they said, *yes.* Instantly, they get your amazing freebie, satisfying their desire for something valuable and providing instant gratification. Their brain became happy.

With subsequent emails, they continued to say "yes" by opening and reading them, especially if they were well-written.

Side note: Your email service provider's analytics can provide insights into **open rates** and **click-through rates**. Ideally, you want subscribers to open your messages, read them in their entirety, and click on the links within. Each small action they take is another "yes" in your favor.

So, go ahead and include helpful links where appropriate, directing them to reputable articles or useful YouTube videos. People appreciate receiving little gifts, and each interaction contributes to their brain's happiness.

With every email they receive from you, their brain becomes even happier. It's all part of building a strong relationship, where saying "yes" becomes increasingly effortless. By the time you're ready to make a bigger ask, such as signing up for a webinar, they'll be quick to say "yes" once again. This is because you've taken the time to establish yourself as trustworthy and credible, nurturing their trust throughout the email sequence.

Bonus Pro Tip

Remember, just as a first date can be the start of a beautiful relationship, your free offer is an opportunity to cultivate a long-lasting connection with your audience. So, don't leave them hanging! Take the time to develop an engaging and informative email sequence that will not only keep them interested but also nurture a relationship built on trust, value, and mutual benefit.

By crafting a well-thought-out email sequence, you can provide additional information, insights, and resources related to the initial free offer. This not only demonstrates your expertise and commitment but also keeps your brand top-of-mind for your audience. It shows that you genuinely care about their needs and want to help them achieve their goals.

Weekly Blogs

Starting in the late 90's blogs were a primary source to generate website traffic and increase revenue. Blogging was new and trending. But it's 2023 so everyone's asking, "Are blogs still relevant to my online marketing?"

The answer is yes-but.

Yes, blogs are still relevant to your online marketing strategy. Yes, they are important tools to build your authority in your field of expertise, to help you stand out from your competition as a thought leader, and to build trust with your reader.

But they need to be done differently than they were a decades ago. To effectively grow your business with blogs you need to update your method to the current trends because so much has changed.

11 Components For A Stelllar Blog

Today to have a killer blog you must understand and include:

- Search Engine Optimization
- Attention-grabbing headlines and subheaders
- Targeted keywords and long-tail keywords
- Quality, high-value content
- Long-form writing; 1400 words or more
- Links/linking
- Cited credible sources
- Proper text formatting including using H1 text style for titles and H2 text styles for subtitles
- Images
- Strong CTA's
- Post 1-2 blogs per week

I know. It's a long list. Please, don't be intimidated. I'm going to break it down and explain it all to you. Be assured that you don't have to hit every one of these all the time to write effectively. Start to incorporate as many of these practices as possible. It's necessary if your goal is to stand out in the sea of content so do your best.

As you start to incorporate what you learn here today you will see the difference it makes in your long term marketing strategy. Blogs, when written well, will build momentum over time. Sure, they make a big impact when they first go out to your subscribers, but they also gain momentum organically on the web as long as they are on your site.

Search engines like Google, Bing, and Yahoo! have methods of "crawling websites" to determine how different web pages will rank in their search engine results. Blogs, as well as other content, will continue to be spotted and ranked according to the current standards.

Do you want to be on the first page of Google without having to pay for ads? Of course! Everyone does. So let's keep learning how you can learn to write an amazing blog.

How To Write Killer Blogs

Let's start with the first three items on our list; SEO, headlines, and keywords.

SEO, or search engine optimization, is always something to be aware of when it comes to creating online content. Your web developer uses it on the back end of your site to help you stand out already. Most likely by location or specialty. To stand apart, you must understand and use SEO in all of your website content, including your blogs.

Here's why it's important.

SEO is the process of incorporating keywords and phrases that you want to rank for in search engines. For example, let's say you're writing a blog to explain the benefits of infrared light therapy to treat joint pain. What keywords can you use in your writing to optimize the chances of your blog being found by search engines?

Here are two possible headline titles. Tell me which one you think will be more effective at attracting leads.

Red Light Therapy is Now Available!
Or,
Relieve Your Chronic Joint Pain Today With Red Light Therapy

Which would you pick? I hope you picked the second one because the first title is generic and vague. No one looking for help to relieve their joint pain is going to type in red light therapy into an address bar. They don't know what that is yet. Instead, they will search for words and phrases that *describe their symptoms*. This is key!

The second title has words and phrases that someone would actually type into a search bar seeking help.

Think Like Your Ideal Customer or Client

This is where you need to forget what you think you know. Instead, think like your potential client. What would *they* type into a search engine if they were suffering from chronic joint pain?

Maybe-
- Chronic joint pain relief
- Joint pain relief
- Joint pain
- Pain relief for joint pain
- Relief for joint pain

While these phrases are similar, they are typical variations one would search for. That makes it more effective for search engine optimization. These are the keywords you want to use in your headline, subheadings, and text.

Another point to make is that the second title is more attention-grabbing than the first. If you want them to read your blog, you have to get their attention. Make them curious, stir their interests.

Bonus Pro Tip

Blogs can become part of your email sequence. For example, in your nurturing email sequence, you can introduce the blog topic you just wrote about. Include a link that they can click on that brings them to your website and read that blog. It's simple, easy, and takes care of two things at once. It's a blog. It's an email.

And…

It can also be used in part for ads, promotions or printed materials. Believe me when I say a well-written blog is worth every penny.

Leverage Social Media

I know you probably don't have time or energy left at the end of the day, week, or month to spend on planning out marketing content for your business. I get it. So the best, *but not free option,* is to hire a pro as soon as you can because this is a specialized area of advertising.

However, if you want to keep your hard-earned cash, there are some things you can do yourself. This is a DIY guide after all! So here is what you can do for free.

Create your own branded ads using <u>Canva</u> (or a similar platform) and upload them to your social media accounts. If you've already learned how to build a website, this will be a cinch. It's an intuitive software that will guide you through the process of customizing templates for professional designs to promote your business.

You can keep it simple and use their automated scheduler to post a month's worth of content or more.

Not sure what to post? Here's what's trending now.

- Keep it simple and post helpful info your target audience would love and benefit from.
- Tease out a juicy quote from your latest blog and include a link
- Remember to acknowledge holidays important to your audience.
- Share glimpses into your daily life and include pics of your pets, tell a funny story that happened if you want.
- Give a message of encouragement or …
- Tell them a lesson you learned the hard way so that they gain wisdom without the trial.

The point is to share anything that will help your readers connect with you as a person. Remember connection builds trust. Trusting you is one step closer to buying your offer.

Bonus Pro Tip

First, remember, you're not only selling your product or services–you're also selling yourself. People are looking for providers they can trust and relate to. Be yourself.

Secondly, if you're an older person like me, say in the over 40 or 50 club, it's kind of hard to change the mindset we were raised with. That mindset that says everything has to be proper, cleaned up, and polished. The idea that you must always keep your business life separate from your personal life is outdated. What worked a few decades ago is obsolete in today's market.

People want to see the real you as much as they want to see you shine in the zone of your expertise. Get used to mixing the two together.

Assess Your Website

That's right. I said, give your website a check-up. Especially if it's been more than a year since you or your web developer has taken a close look at it. Chances are you're losing money because your website is not performing as well as you think.

If potential clients and customers have a bad user experience when they land on your site, they will click away from your site in *seconds!* Don't lose them.

If it's been five years or longer, you should seriously consider whether a redesign is in order so that your site stays current with the trends.

Here's a list of what you should look for.

Check every page of your website for these six things. Let's start with a couple of easy ones and work our way up.

1) Outdated Information

It probably doesn't need to be said, but I'd be remiss if I failed to mention this. Outdated information of any sort is a no-no. Anything from dated images to staff bios of people who no longer work at your company, search for outdated information and bring it up to date.

2) Broken Links

Find them and fix them. Period. Yes, this means you will have to check them all one at a time. Tedious yes, but absolutely necessary if you want to look professional. From your home navigation bar to blog posts with outbound links, check them all.

3) Website Load Time

Certain types of content will bog down your site if your website. So be sure your site is hosted by a great platform. Check every page of your site. Sometimes your homepage is fine, but maybe your product page is lagging because you have tons of HD images. Get the upgrades you need for lightning-fast page upload times.

If not, lagging load times **will** cost you. There is no question. You may have great products but if your customer is waiting for a page to load they are going to get frustrated and you will lose sales.

If your website has slow load times, find out why and fix it. If you don't know how talk to your web developer. Let a pro bring your entire website up to speed.

4) Content

Content refers to inbound marketing. Essentially it is everything on your website, your words, images, articles, blogs, etc. It's also anything you put out on social media or in ads. Content is all the info you use to communicate with your ideal clients and customers. So it is important that you give thought to what it is you want to say.

So the question is, is your content and your marketing message clear? Are you conveying a clear and consistent message throughout all your marketing assets?

If not, you're likely confusing your prospects. Now let me tell you the bad news about that. If your ideal customers are confused, you are definitely losing money!

Your message must be simple and straightforward. And it must remain consistent throughout your website. Every page should, in some way, repeat your core message. Tell them over and over:

- Who you are
- What do you do
- What problem will you solve
- How can they get it

Follow this up by giving them a very clear call to action (CTA) and a button or link to click to complete the call to action. For example, you really want to sell a product or service. Tell them to 'buy now' or 'click here.' Make it obvious what you want them to do next. Then give them a fast and easy way to do it.

5) Website Design & Navigation

Have you ever been frustrated with a website because you couldn't find a navigation tab to take you to the information you wanted? Or the design was so full of pictures, videos, and cute fonts and backgrounds were so busy that your eyes and your brain hurt?

Don't overwhelm your site visitors with too much extra fluff. And be sure your design is clean, simple, and easy to navigate through. Less is often better.

6) Smart Design for Desktops, Smart Phones, & Tablets

Be sure to view your website on all the available platforms. You'd be surprised at how great your site looks on a desktop and how awful it is on a smartphone. Sometimes images get cropped wrong and text gets cut off or squished together. Even overlapping! It makes it impossible for someone to read or use it.

Take a look at each platform type. Your website builder should offer you optional views and most of them adapt accordingly, but if they don't, you'll need to do some editing.

It is vital for everything to look and work the way it's supposed to. Again, it's all about the user's experience.

Bonus Pro Tip

If it's been five years or longer, you should seriously consider whether a redesign is in order so that your site stays current with the trends. Take a look at it from your site visitors' point of view. Are your images, color scheme or design out of date? How does it measure up to your competitors?

You and I both know that just because something is shiny and new doesn't make it better or the best. But first impressions are just that…first impressions. Make yours the best that you can!

It's Your Turn!

Congratulations! You made it to the end of your first marketing how-to book!

Now it's your turn. It's time to take action and implement what you've learned. The strategies I've given you are designed to empower you so you can take control of your marketing efforts and achieve success without the need to hire an expert.

You can transform your marketing, reach your target audience more effectively, and grow your business. And you can keep your hard-earned cash!

Here's a quick recap of the 5 key strategies you just learned:

1. **<u>Build Your Email List:</u>** Don't underestimate the power of an engaged email list. Capture the interest of your website visitors by offering them valuable opt-ins and creating a permission-based relationship with your prospects. Focus on providing genuine value, nurturing the conversation, and building trust with your subscribers.

2. **Email Sequencing:** Utilize email sequencing or sales funnels to deepen your connection with your audience. Engage them with a series of well-crafted emails that provide valuable information, insights, and solutions to their problems. By consistently delivering value, you can establish yourself as a trusted authority and guide them toward taking desired actions.

3. **Post Weekly Blogs:** Establish your expertise and build trust by consistently posting long-form, well-optimized blogs on your website. Regularly sharing informative content will not only improve your search engine rankings but also attract and engage your target audience. Incorporate your blog posts into your email sequence to further enhance your relationship with your subscribers.

4. **Post on Social Media:** Leverage the power of social media to promote your business without breaking the bank. Create branded ads using user-friendly platforms like Canva and share helpful information, personal stories, and engaging content that resonates with your audience. Remember to be

authentic and showcase your personality to connect with your followers.

5. **Give Your Website a Check-Up:** Ensure your website is up to par by regularly reviewing and updating its content, fixing broken links, optimizing load times, and ensuring a clear and consistent marketing message. A well-designed and user-friendly website will enhance the user experience, boost credibility, and improve conversion rates.

By implementing these strategies, you will:

- Effectively reach and engage your target audience
- Build trust, and
- Establish yourself as an industry expert

Remember, success requires action, so don't hesitate to put these ideas into practice. Embrace the opportunity to connect with your audience, provide value, and you will achieve your business goals.

You hold the reins of your marketing efforts. Embrace the power of these strategies, adapt them to your unique business needs, and you'll start seeing the results. And the best part is that your hard-earned cash can stay with you as you navigate the world of digital marketing.

Here's something else you gain in the process. Knowledge. So when you are ready to hire a professional copywriter to help with your marketing, you'll know they are legit when they implement these key strategies. You'll know what to look for!

Remember, you have something valuable to offer, and with the right marketing plan and the perfect words, you will reach the people who need what you have and they will be eager to invest in your business.

May these strategies guide you toward greater success. Best of luck on your marketing journey!

Begin Your Marketing Plan

The following pages are to help you begin putting a marketing plan together to grow your business. They are simply prompts to help guide you through the thought process.

You will begin by listing 1-3 of your business goals. Next, you'll break down each goal into individual steps you'll need to take in order to achieve that goal. The last step is to set target dates for when you will have each completed.

Don't worry. You can definitely change this as you go. As a matter of fact, I'd be quite surprised if you hit every goal on your actual target dates. Most of us bite off a little more than we can chew! So, it's important to give yourself some grace and make adjustments as needed.

The main thing is to start somewhere, make a plan, and begin to execute it. You will reach your goals if you work on them.

Business Goals:

Get specific on your top three business goals and write them down here. Don't overthink this. You can always change this later.

> **1.**

> **2.**

> **3.**

What steps need to happen for Goal 1 to be achieved?

_____

_____

_____

_____

_____

_____

What steps need to happen for Goal 2 to be achieved?

_____

_____

_____

_____

_____

_____

What steps need to happen for Goal 3 to be achieved?

_____

_____

_____

_____

_____

_____

Notes:

Timeline: Set achieveable goals

Completion Date for Goal 1: _____

Completion Date for Goal 2: _____

Completion Date for Goal 3: _____

These are *your goals* to grow *your business*. You are serious about making them happen so make achieving these goals your priority. Think non-negotiable. Mark your calendar with these dates and place in a prominent spot where you will see them daily and take the steps to reach your goals.

And…

Drumroll please.

Celebrate your progress!

It's just as important as everthing you've just learned. Even small wins along the way shoudl be recognized, shared with others, and celebrated. This is the good stuff that keeps you motivated to push through on those days when it's been a challenge to meet your goals. You and both know those days will come so, prepare for them. It will make your life so much easier.

Notes:

Additional Resouces

Compiled below is a list of resources you will find helpful. They will enhance your understanding and knowledge of marketing even further when you are ready to tackle these topics. Each resource is packed with practical advice you can actually do yourself. They also give you the perspective of an expert enabling you to delve deeper into the world of marketing and take your DIY skills to the next level.

Learn How SEO Works &How To Make It Work For You

Drive More Traffic To Your Website By Doing Just 3 Things

Why Being Yourself Is The Best Marketing Strategy

Should I Be Using Email Campaigns?

All articles can be found at www.kellygawittagency.com/blog

For more information on marketing and copywriting services, or to learn about how you can work with me, go to:

www.kellygawitt.com